Crysta

CW01498345

ULTIMATE LIST OF CRYSTALS AND THEIR USES, CRYSTAL HEALING AND ENERGY FIELDS

By Mia Rose

Table Of Contents

Preview of Chakras for Beginners

Check Out My Other Books

About the Author

Introduction

I want to thank you and congratulate you for downloading the book, *"Crystals, The Ultimate Guide to Crystal Healing"*.

This book contains proven steps and strategies on how to use crystals to heal both physical and mental conditions along with techniques to care for crystals, choose crystals and the benefits of different types of precious and semi-precious stones.

Thanks again for downloading this book, I hope you enjoy it!

Chapter 1

Clear As Crystal; Crystal Healing Facts

If you are reading this book on an electronic device (e-book reader, computer, smart-phone) then you're already utilizing the power of crystals. Even if you're reading it in a more physical form the process by which a print copy has been produced will have involved some form of technology in which crystals played a part!

While using crystals within a technological setting may be a standard part of our lives – even if we are not aware of just how many of our existing technological advancements depend on them – some people find it a more difficult concept to understand that crystals can do more than store information or be used to transmit or create electricity.

In fact, crystal healing has long been practiced in many traditional settings – particularly in religious and healing traditions in India and the Far East. In the last century this practice has become more widely established in the west and is now accepted by many as an integral part of many healing traditions.

How Does Crystal Healing Work?

Energy is a force that resonates and radiates throughout everything in the universe. Without energy nothing could exist and our own bodies are vibrant with this essential life force. Ill-health is, in part, a manifestation of imbalances within the natural energy field that operates around us. Where these imbalances occur it is possible to use different kinds of energy to re-balance them. Hunger can be dissipated with the energy in our food and cancerous tumors can be dissipated by the energy from radiation (radiotherapy). Everything around us also emanates energy and crystals are unique in that the energy that radiates from them is stable and remains constant. Crystals are formed in patterns and structures which can be used to re-balance or re-tune our own energy fields.

While it is important to take professional medical advice if you suffer from any condition, throughout the ages, crystals have been used to heal and to maintain the balance of our own energy field. The raw energy contained in crystals is easy to attune to; it is formed from the same essential patterns that create all life in the universe. In crystal healing, specific qualities of different crystal structures are used to tune our own energy fields to their correct frequency. As with radiation (which is just light, after all) crystals can radiate energy that can help us to heal and also provide protection from ill-health.

Finding Your Crystals

Crystals have different qualities and even individual crystals of the same type will resonate differently on a very subtle level. Finding the right crystals for you is actually very easy – in fact the crystals will be more likely to find you! Simply holding a crystal in your hand will, with some practice, identify if it's the right crystal for you. In reality all crystals have beneficial qualities and as you start to work with crystals your choices can be more specific. Attuning yourself to crystals can take time – though for some individuals it is a faster process than for others. In this book we'll take you through some simple steps which will help on your journey including a close look at how to care for crystals and meditations to use when working with them.

If you have a very specific issue which you wish to address with crystals then finding an appropriate crystal which has links to that condition will be useful. However, intuition plays a large part in crystal healing and simply holding a crystal in your hand can often indicate if it is the right crystal for you. In this book we'll also take a look at some of the most popular crystals and their uses but always look to your reaction to a crystal to decide whether it can benefit you in anyway.

Crystals and the Chakras

Crystal healing is strongly associated with the concept of Chakras. These are traditional "energy" points identified in a number of healing systems, particularly those with roots in India and the Far East. The Chakras are understood as spinning, energy vortexes where our own individual energy field connects to the wider universe and to the greater energy that flows through it. Crystals are used for their own very strong qualities at focusing this energy to direct it into relevant energy points within the body and they can balance or stimulate the individual Chakras. For those new to energy healing, the recipe for success is simple; to address specific issues identify the Chakra that controls the particular bodily functions (or emotions) with which there is a problem and then use the crystals associated with the same conditions or energy. The seven primary Chakras are as follows;

1. The Base Chakra, or the Root Chakra is located at the base of the spine. This is related to physicality, grounding and a sense of belonging. It is associated with the color red and with our basic physical needs such as food and shelter.

2. Colored Orange, the Sacral Chakra is located a couple of inches below the navel and is linked to our relations with others, including romantic and sexual relationships. This Chakra is related to emotional issues, sexuality and our ability to experience pleasure.

3. The Solar Plexus Chakra, colored yellow is located in the upper portion of the abdomen around the stomach. This chakra relates to our sense of self, to confidence and our ability to be open and honest.

4. The Heart Chakra, colored green, is located in the center of our chest around the heart itself. It relates to our ability to love in the wider sense, our sense of respect for those around us and our ability to give of ourselves. The chakra governs health issues related to

stress and to physical issues related to both the heart and lungs.

5. The Throat Chakra, colored blue, is located around our throats! It is related to communication, expression and creativity. Physically it can relate to throat and breathing issues, colds and flu.

6. The Third Eye Chakra, colored indigo, is located between the eyes on the forehead. This chakra is linked to wisdom, intuition and to decision making. It is related to mental issues and anxiety disorders including a range of depressive illnesses.

7. The Crown Chakra; this chakra is colored violet (although considered to be colorless by some). It is located at the very top of our head. This chakra is related to spirituality, to bliss and to a connection with the wider universal forces. Illnesses including Alzheimer's, headaches, dizziness, depression and more serious mental illnesses such as schizophrenia are linked with this chakra.

Colors and Crystals

Colors have strong magical and healing associations in their own right and can be found playing a role in many different magical traditions from candle magic to chakra healing. The basic associations with each color are relevant in crystal healing as well, and these are described below:

- Red; signifies both fire and blood and is associated with both anger and focus. Passion, action and purification are also strongly associated with the color. Achieving grace through purification is also strongly linked to this color and it has powerful associations with radical change and healing.

- Orange; this color indicates spirituality, bravery, inspirational spontaneity, sociability, intelligence and contentment. Achieving balance and harmony in life is a strong feature of the associations with this color and it can be beneficial at establishing a sense of contentment.

- Yellow; a very individual color, yellow signifies creativity, focus, inspiration, ingenuity and inventiveness. It is associated with the sun, for obvious reasons, and was the imperial color in China where garments of yellow were worn by the Emperor alone. It is associated strongly with authority, power and strength.

- Green; this color has many complex associations and it's the color that we see all around us. It symbolizes the earth, fertility and, in many cultures, has strong associations with the concept of the divine. Benevolence, temperance and empathy are common associations with this color and it is also strongly associated with good luck.

- Blue; the color of the heavens and the oceans, blue represent tranquility, peace, rest, recovery and good health. Associations with the sky mean that it linked to the element of air and to clarity of thought, while associations with oceans link it to emotions and particularly to serenity and peace.

- Indigo; a deeper form of blue, this color is associated with many similar attributes to that of blue but on a deeper level. Deep intellectual thought, serenity and peace of mind on the deepest level are all associations that come with this color. Wisdom and intuition are both strongly associated with indigo, as is the concept of justice.

- Violet; abundance, good fortune, plenty and leadership qualities are often associated with this color. In the west it was the color of emperors (as with yellow in the east) and many perceive this color to have similar connotations for this reason. Wealth and power are often associated with violet.

- White; a complex color that is associated with both clarity and purity but also with coldness and distance. White is, in fact, the absence of color and has associations with completion, the beginning and ends of cycles in all areas of life. It is the color of virginity, or youth, yet it is also the color of mourning, in many cultures, signifying death, old age and loss.

- Black; like white, this is another complex color with many associations. Again, used in mourning, it can also be associated with strength, prudence, wisdom and loyalty. Black is also the color of night and this creates associations with both magic and dreams along with intuitive knowledge and hidden knowledge.

Crystal Care and Cleaning

Crystals vibrate with energy and they can also store energy from all around them. They are not discriminating when it comes to absorbing vibrations and will pick up both positive and negative energies from the environment in which they are placed. For this reason it's important to take good care of your crystals and to ensure that they remain filled with positive, healing energy. Cleansing a crystal and "programming" it is a simple process and can be done in a number of ways. The two most common ways use water to help clean away negative vibrations. Some practitioners recommend using spring water (which is ideal) but a basic cleanse can be completed using running water of any kind (including from a tap!). Below are three common methods used to cleanse crystals.

1. Hold your stone under a source of running water; this can be a stream or tap, or water poured from a bottle or jug. Only use cold or slightly warm water, never hot. As the water flows over the stone simply visualize the negative energy and vibrations flowing away from the crystal and pure, positive energies flowing from your body into the stone. Do not dry using a towel or cloth but leave to dry naturally in the sun.

2. Place a bowl of water on a windowsill and add sea-salt giving it a good stir to ensure the salt is dissolved. Place your crystal in the bowl making sure that it is completely covered with water. Ideally do this at the start of the day as the sun rises and leave until midday when the sun is at its full height. Then remove the crystal and dry in the sunlight, as mentioned in the first method.

3. For quartz crystals, in particular, simply burying them in the earth is recommended by many practitioners. The planet itself is made up of approximately one third quartz and the magnetic energy fields that this creates will help to cleanse your crystals in the most natural way. This both cleans and energizes your crystals. This method can be used for any crystal but is most effective for quartz of all kinds.

Programming Crystals

Crystal healing and meditation works by using the crystal's ability to store and focus energy. Crystals naturally pick up vibrations from around them but by programming your crystals you can focus the crystal's energy on a particular purpose. Once you have programmed a particular crystal the programming will remain and the energy that the crystal emits will continue to provide focus on the matter in question. If you wish, you can "clear" this programming and/or "reprogram" the crystal as desired. Stones can be used for any purpose, for healing or protection, for luck, for love or for financial gain.

As each type of precious or semi-precious stone has different associations you should choose the most appropriate stone for your specific goal. Before you program a stone, or stones, you must be careful to clearly define your goal and the purpose for which you wish the stone to work. Properly programmed a crystal will be focused and powerful but clarity is crucial; remember that the stone cannot "think" for itself, if you are not sure of your own intention then this uncertainty will be fed into the stone!

To focus your thoughts simply think through what you require from the stone and write down this intention in a single sentence. Keep the sentence as short as possible with only one main point. Once you have this thought clearly in your mind you can begin to program your crystal.

Simply sit in a quiet space where you will not be interrupted and hold the stone in your hand (use your left hand if you are left handed or right if right handed). Some people like to burn an incense associated with the same purpose with which they wish to program the stone but, at first, it may be better to limit the distractions around you.

Focus on the stone, study it and feel its weight in your hand. Allow yourself to sense its energy, vibration and power. Gradually you will begin to feel a sense of harmony with the stone as it attunes to your energy and you to its. At this point the stone is ready to be programmed.

Deepen your focus on the stone and say out loud what purpose you wish the stone to fulfill. You can use your written statement if you wish and repeat this several times as you continue to focus on the crystal in your palm. Remain sitting quietly for a moment or two, still focused on the crystal and the thought with which you are programming it. Feel the energy in the crystal pulsing in your hand and imagine the outcome that you wish to achieve.

Once the stone is programmed it will retain the energy you have placed into it. You may wish to place the stone under your pillow or either carry it with you or place it in a specific location in your home. Crystals can pass their energy into other crystals if they touch, so you may wish to wrap the crystal in plain cloth to ensure that messages, energies and intentions don't become mixed. If this does happen by accident you'll need to cleanse your stones as described above and then reprogram them.

Chapter 2

Basic Meditation Techniques

Meditation is an ancient technique found in nearly every religious tradition – big or small – and in every culture throughout history. It can remove stress, create calm and is recognized as a treatment for depression, anxiety and many related disorders by doctors and the medical establishments in many different countries. The full health benefits of meditation have not been fully researched but medical experts agree that it can not only help with mental health but be beneficial for many physical conditions and is even a natural pain killer!

Meditating with crystals is the perfect way to not only program the crystals themselves but also to focus your own mind on a specific goal. Depending on your intentions or needs, you should choose an appropriate crystal for the meditation (see the section on types of crystals later in this book). In this chapter we'll take a look at basic meditations that can be used as a framework to meditate with crystals and can be adapted for different purposes.

Meditation Basics

Always meditate in a quiet space, where you will not be interrupted. Some people choose to meditate with candles, incense or music and all of these can be helpful in achieving a state of relaxation. Choose which, if any, works for you and try different methods until you find the most effective "tools".

Wear loose fitting clothing (or none at all) and ensure that the room (or space) is at a comfortable heat. As you meditate your body's processes will slow and you may feel colder.

Remaining physically comfortable is important when meditating; you can meditate for a few moments or much longer, especially as you practice, so minimizing any possible distractions, including physical ones, is essential.

After meditating it can be important to bring yourself firmly back into the real world. Have a hot drink and snack, play some louder music, go for a walk in the fresh air and sunlight (or wind and rain!). Ground yourself back in the real world in whatever way suits you best.

Basic Mindfulness Meditation

Mindfulness is a meditation technique that has roots in Buddhist practice and it is one of the most common meditation techniques used today. Mindfulness meditation can be conducted anywhere, anytime and is a way of simply relaxing and fully experiencing the moment. You can practice mindfulness meditation at home, work or in the park (though be sure to practice relaxation techniques in a safe place). It's a good type of meditation for those learning to meditate and will help you to develop your skills in order to be able to conduct deeper, more effective forms of meditation. The following basic mindfulness meditation can last for as long, or short, a period as you require.

1. Focus your attention on the moment; stand or sit upright and close your eyes.

2. Ask yourself "what am I experiencing right now? What thoughts, what feelings, what physical sensations?"

3. Acknowledge each thought, emotion, sensation, good and bad alike.

4. Gradually redirect your attention to your breathing. Simply focus on the sensation of the air entering your lungs and leaving your lungs. Breath in through your nose and out through your mouth.

5. Allow your sense of awareness to expand once more, to each physical sensation, sounds and your own presence in the space in which you are meditating. Continue to breath regularly and deeply.

6. As thoughts surface, note them and move on. Do not allow one thought to distract you but continue to focus on the present, physical moment.

7. Conclude by stretching, yawning, taking a deep breath in and opening your eyes as you expel the air from your lungs.

Pyramid Meditation

This meditation will help you to learn to visualize – an important part of meditation, healing and crystal healing. Use it to practice and develop both your meditation skills and your crystal healing skills.

1. Hold your crystal in either hand – whichever feels "right" and sit on the floor in a cross legged position.

2. Close your eyes and take three deep breaths, breathing in through the nose and filling the lungs. Hold each breath to the count of three. Expel the air from your lungs in a short breath through your mouth. Repeat this process two more times. You may feel a little light-headed but this is normal.

3. Count backwards from nine to one taking a breath at each number. Do this slowly and rhythmically and as you do so remind yourself to return to full consciousness in ten or fifteen minutes. Your mind and internal body clock should do this automatically but if you prefer you can set an alarm.

4. Continue to breath at the rate you have established in step three and with your eyes closed begin to focus on the color associated with your aims. This should be the same color as the crystal you are using.

5. Visually, in your mind, construct a pyramid, with the tip located a foot or so above your head. The four points should fall on the floor around you, two behind and two in front. Imagine the color flooding this pyramid.

6. If you are using the meditation for healing, feel the color washing around you within the pyramid and focus it towards the area you wish to heal, or the source of pain.

7. Towards the end of the session, either when your own internal alarm begins to bring you back to fuller consciousness or the alarm you have set rings, simply focus on your breathing and count back from one to nine and open your eyes at nine.

8. Visually imagine the pyramid dissolve around you and focus for a moment or two on the crystal in your hand. Once you feel you have fully returned to consciousness end the meditation and ground yourself back in the real world.

Chapter 3

Crystal Attributes in Detail

All crystals can be used in crystal healing – including precious stones. While you may not wish to start a collection of rubies, diamonds, emeralds or sapphires it's possible that you already have some jewelery that features one or more of them. While loose stones are better for crystal healing purposes you can still focus energy on jewelery pieces and this has the advantage that you can carry the positively charged energy with you as you go! If you do choose to purchase small precious gemstones for use in crystal healing they can be very powerful stones indeed. In this section we'll take a tour of the big four!

Precious Gemstones

Diamonds

The traditional image of diamonds is of the crystal clear variety but diamonds do come in a wide range of colors. If you choose to use diamonds in crystal healing the different colors will have associations of their own. The most common color variations are pink, yellow, blue and black.

Diamonds symbolize clarity and purity; they are strongly associated with love and partnership, bringing clarity and honesty into relationships. In crystal healing they can be used to establish strong, deep bonds in personal relationships, to create fidelity and trust between partners. The gem is also associated with abundance, wealth and great energy. In crystal healing diamonds are particularly powerful at helping to create the atmosphere for accumulation of wealth and success – both of the lasting kind. There is great strength in diamonds and this is one of their key associations, stimulation individuality, creativity and brilliance of mind.

Rubies

These fiery stones are full to the brim with explosive energy! They are associated with passion, change, sensuality and lust. In healing terms they are excellent at dispelling lethargy, at improving both circulation and breathing. They encourage self-expression and innovative thought, so are useful stones to carry when studying or taking exams. The association that these stones have with fire is also in the sense of fires in which all manner of things are forged and this can make them useful stones to use for good luck with creating new things – both physical and intellectual. Invention, innovation and the ability to bring about great change are all encapsulated in the qualities that this gemstone can impart.

Emeralds

Keenly associated with love, luck and fertility, this stone can create a powerful healing affect in all of these areas. It creates an atmosphere of loyalty in close personal relationships and encourages friendship and respect. Strongly associated with the earth, with growth and with sustenance, the green colored emerald is a perfect stone for use in any healing where positive growth and change is required. Emerald is associated with luck too and for anyone needing a little unexpected and surprise assistance in life or love this is the stone to use! Carrying or wearing an emerald offers both protection and guidance and it is often associated with clairvoyance – both the physic ability and also the practical ability to see things as they really are.

Sapphires

Traditionally seen as a deep rich blue, these stones, like diamonds also come in a startling array of colors. Blue, yellow, black, pink, white, green and indigo are all variations on the theme of sapphires. The stone itself is strongly associated with wisdom and imparts a deep knowledge to those who use it. The different shades may address different areas of life and knowledge but all impart a deeply rooted understanding of that area. Sapphire is also known for its ability to create balance and harmony in both the body and mind. It can be a very healing stone which can be used to bring the body back into an equilibrium after an illness or to calm the mind. Bringers of joy and serenity, sapphires are also known for their ability to attract gifts, to make dreams come true and to find fulfillment.

Crystals

Crystals used in healing can be sourced cheaply and easily. Many can be bought online but it's often wise to buy crystals in a real-world store. This give you the opportunity to feel the energy within the crystal and evaluate whether it is the right crystal for you. Sometimes, when searching for new crystals one will "jump" out at you, which is a good sign that you would benefit strongly from the stone. Online stores do, however, offer a great deal of convenience and can be a great way to source new crystals as you become more experienced working with them.

There is a massive range of different types of crystal and finding the right crystals to work with is largely a matter of personal choice and specific needs. In this section we'll take a look at some of the most commonly used crystals that have long been used for healing. A number of crystals come in different forms and in this section we'll look at the uses of different crystals and their sub-forms.

Agates

Agates have a soothing and calming effect and can be used in a great range of healing applications. They come in several different forms each with their own unique qualities and appearance.

- Standard agate is a beautiful stone, with unusual patterns running through it. Agate creates inner strength, poise and a sense of serenity. It works slowly, bringing peace and self-acceptance, making it a good stone for work on emotional issues. All agates are believed to bring analytical abilities and the ability to solve problems in a practical way.

- Crazy-lace, or Mexican Agate, creates confidence and a sense of well being. It relieves emotional pain and stress and will attract positive energies and people into your life. Physically it can foster energy in the major organs and remove energy blockages in the Chakras.

- Fire agate is a very protective stone. An excellent stone to carry with you, it offers a shield against negative thoughts and intentions in others. Fire agate brings a sense of safety, security and strength. Physically it is ideal for healing stomach problems, cravings and helps in the treatment of addictions of all kinds.

- Moss agate comes in a beautifully patterned, subtle green color. As with any green stone it is associated with luck, growth and prosperity. It is a stone of fresh starts and should be worn or programmed to aid with any new project in life. Physically it will help with recovery from injuries, speed recovery from colds and flu and is believed to be good for reducing pain and inflammation.

- Tree agate is a striking white stone with green markings and is closely associated with nature. It helps to create strong structures in life – be they relationships, careers or homes. It is a nurturing stone and offers protection to children, animals and plants. Like a tree, the power in tree agate is slow acting and if used it should be carried for a long time to reap the full benefits.

Amber

Amber is not strictly speaking a crystal! It's the fossilized remains of ancient tree resin and often contains fragments of vegetation or even insects. Although not a crystal as such it's a powerful healing stone and is commonly used in crystal healing. In healing it is believed to be extremely powerful at drawing away negative energy both from physical or emotional sources. Amber soaks away illness and negative emotions and turns them into positive and good health. Physical ailments with which amber can provide relief include stomach disorders, kidney and bladder problems and liver problems.

Amethyst

This beautiful purple stone is highly protective, warding off evil in all its many forms. Traditionally amethyst was believed to ward off nightmares and placing a charged crystal under the pillow or by your bed is recommended. For physical illnesses, amethyst is commonly used to treat headaches, tension and to reduce inflammation (particularly bruising or swelling). Amethyst is also believed to be a powerful stone for combating addictions.

Bloodstone

This is a dark stone with flecks of red running through it and is sometimes known as Heliotrope. It is strongly associated with the blood – with circulation and heart function. It brings grounding and protection and is believed to promote strong friendships. Physically it is used in healing to address liver, kidney and bladder problems, as it aids the removal of toxins from the body. Bloodstone is also believed to have soothing and calming qualities and is commonly placed by the bed to aid natural sleep.

Calcite

Another crystal which comes in a wide range of colors, the general properties of calcite are calming and refreshing.

- Blue calcite is generally light and milky in color, it is restful, peaceful and calming, soothing the body and mind. Physically it is good for lung disorders, breathing related conditions and throat conditions.

- Green calcite is bright, minty, refreshing looking stone. This stone provides strength in difficult situations, mental sharpness and balance. In healing it is used to calm fevers, aid recovery from minor burns and is a good immune system booster.

- Orange calcite is believed to banish negative energy, thoughts and emotions. It is an excellent stone to create positivity in your life and is known to bring energy, laughter and joy into your life. In healing it can be used to treat intestinal disorders and is also commonly used to combat depression by virtue of its positive vibrations.

- Red calcite brings energy in abundance and also promotes optimism. Additionally it also gives the ability to combat fears and remove obstacles in life. Red is associated with the base Chakra and this stone can be effective at treating lower limb disorders and hip problems. It's an excellent all round energizer and can help those with fatigue-related illnesses.

Citrine

Like all crystals colored with a hint of orange this stone promotes positivity. It's great for finding inspiration, tapping into creativity and building self-confidence. The stone is believed to help those wearing it to achieve their goals, particularly personal development goals. It's also believed to attract good luck with money in general. Citrine is a good crystal to help lift depression or anxiety related disorders and physically is a crystal which will promote good health in general and build the immune system.

Fluorite

This crystal is typically banded with different colors. It is believed to assist in the understanding of new ideas and information. Fluorite is a good general healing crystal and is particularly useful at fending off infections, colds or flu. Many healers also ascribe powerful qualities at dealing with inflammation, particularly of the joints, and it's commonly recommended to help those suffering from arthritis.

Garnet

This beautiful red stone resembles the ruby and shares many healing qualities with it's "precious" cousin! This stone protects, energizes and regenerates. Red, often symbolizes life force and, as such, this stone is linked to love and to the sex drive. Historically, associated with the planet Mars, this stone was often found embedded in swords and shields. It offers great power and can be very protective against negativity of all kinds. In healing it is an excellent stone to bring back vitality and confidence and can be particularly useful to those suffering from depression, anxiety or fatigue related illnesses. For anybody dealing with obstacles or facing a "battle" in life, this is the stone to carry or wear.

Hematite

This metallic looking crystal is dark, usually black in color, but has an attractive, silvery sheen to it. This is a truly earthy crystal, being a mineral form of iron oxide. It brings both grounding and inspiration – helping you to think creatively and at the same time keeping your feet firmly planted on the earth. This is a powerful combination and can help to ensure success in any new project. In healing its main properties are helping to restore healthy balance to the blood – being particularly useful for those with anemia. It is also recommended for dealing with problems in the legs – fractures, cramps or foot problems of any kind.

Jade

Long considered sacred, holy and linked to Imperial power in China and the Far East, Jade is a term actually applied to two different crystals; Jadeite and Nephrite. The latter is easier and cheaper to obtain and is a darker, opaque crystal. Jade is imbued with qualities that include promoting independence, strength, courage, wisdom and justice. It is also believed to banish negative thoughts and calm troubled souls. Highly protective, it shares qualities of a luck bringer and fruitful endeavors with many other green stones. For healing it is particularly prized as a balancer of the nervous system and in traditional lore it is used as an aid for fertility and for child-birth.

Jasper

This crystal comes in many and varied forms and colors. All share nurturing and calming qualities and promote strength and tenacity. The energy of the crystal is slow to work and when programing it time should be taken to optimize its potential. For healing purposes carrying jasper, or keeping it close to you, will have the best results.

- Brecciated (Brecceated or Bracciated) Jasper; this stone contains small quantities of Hematite and as such shares grounding qualities. It focuses thought and encourages action; in healing it is used to promote happiness and is useful at combating depression or anxiety.

- Dalmatian Jasper; nurturing and promoting positivity this variety of the stone is commonly used in healing mental and emotional issues. It is also believed to help boost the immune system and clear toxins from the body.

- Red Jasper; combining the nurturing nature of jasper with the combative nature of all red stones, this crystal is said to promote problem solving. Red jasper brings problems to the fore, in order for them to be dealt with quickly. Clearing blockages is a key attribute and providing grounding and a sense of wellbeing are also ascribed to the stone.

- Yellow Jasper; this is a protective stone and an inspirational one. Traditionally believed to provide protection for travelers it is commonly held to be an antidote to travel and motion sickness. In healing this stone is used to release toxins, aid digestion and improve energy levels. Like all Jaspers, this stone works slowly and should be kept close for best effects.

Lapis Lazuli

This is a deep, rich, blue-colored crystal that has been highly prized as a gem throughout history. It is associated with thought and expression, clarity and intellect. Blue has many associations with the skies (or heavens) and the oceans. Both have an intangible element to them, representing spirituality and depth of emotion. This gem can be used to promote self-knowledge and spiritual awareness. In healing it is commonly used to stabilize blood pressure and to alleviate headaches, migraines and to aid with healthy sleep.

Moldavite

The super-crystal of the healing world, moldavite is rare and is believed to have formed when a meteorite crashed to earth some 15 million years ago. This created a localized deposit of glass-like material with a bottle-green color. The energy in moldavite is tangible and is often experienced as a tingling, hot sensation when the crystal is held. Its healing powers are said to include instilling huge amounts of energy and it's also believed to promote psychic powers. For those new to crystal work it is wise to meditate with a grounding, stone such as Hematite, and a crystal that protects, such as garnet, when first working with moldavite.

Moonstone

As the name would suggest this delicate, milky stone is linked closely to the moon! Traditionally this makes it the stone of women, and it's used for helping reduce PMT. It's also recommended for women as they experience the menopause and is believed to create a sense of calm. Links with the moon also include moonstone in the list of stones connected to luck in fertility and childbirth. In healing moonstone is recommended for many stress related conditions including stomach disorders related to emotional stress. The stone is gentle, working with the user to promote healing.

Obsidian

Formed from rapidly cooled volcanic lava, Obsidian comes in a range of colors thanks to the action of different minerals during its formation. The stones are extremely powerful and not everybody is comfortable working with the stone at first. All obsidians are protective but they work very quickly which can, on occasion, be unsettling!

- Black; although protective this stone can bring negative thoughts and emotions to the fore very quickly. It acts in this way to help remove them, but the experience can be painful. To protect against negative energies, black obsidian is, however, very powerful. It will absorb negativity rapidly and should be cleansed regularly. In healing it aids digestion, cramps and joint and muscular strains, including rheumatism and arthritis.

- Gold; this provides protection and clarity and is an excellent problem solving stone. Again, it is likely to bring a problem right to your door in order for you to deal with it! In healing it is recommended for balancing the energy field in the body and is a good general healing stone.

- Silver; this form of obsidian resembles hematite to some extent with a subtle silvery sheen. It is, again, a powerful protector and is generally used to help in meditation, as it is believed to calm and ground at the same time.

- Snow-flake; lightly patterned with white "snowflakes" this obsidian is ideal at protecting from negativity and, particularly, grief. It helps to heal gently, after loss, and will promote positive thinking. In healing this is a stone that is widely used to help with skin conditions and is believed to aid with clearing the complexion.

Peridot

This charming, light green crystal is a powerful healing and cleansing stone. It, like any green stone, is linked to healthy, abundant growth, good luck, fortune and protection. It is also associated with helping to deal with guilt, obsession and addiction. It creates a quiet, calm sense of confidence in the user and promotes self-confidence and honesty. In healing it is strongly linked with matters of the heart, both emotionally and physically.

Quartz

This is probably the best known of all healing crystals and also comes in a range of colors and varieties. It contains all the spectrum of light and, for this reason, is known for its power as a general, heal-all crystal. It will create positivity and will amplify the positive in life. In addition, it can create active problem solving, provide clarity and banish negative thoughts from your mind, also banishing negativity from other people around you. Quartz brings the ability to be incisive, act quickly and with confidence.

- Rose; light, pink and translucent this form of quartz is associated with love, beauty and trust. It promotes positive emotions, banishes jealousy or resentment. In healing it is used to help skin problems (including the ability to soothe burns or blisters), clear the complexion and is also used to deal with heart problems and lung problems.

- Rutilated; this quartz has spikes of golden brown color embedded deep within its structure. The stone is believed to promote vitality, energy and to banish depression. In healing it is used to combat phobias and fears and is strongly linked with healing depression. Its ability to rejuvenate is believed to help with healing exhaustion (physical and mental) and is a useful stone for athletes.

- Smoky quartz has similar attributes to rutilated quartz and is excellent for banishing depression, fears or anxieties. The "anti-stress" crystal, this form of quartz will also alleviate physical stress and applying it to an area of pain will help to reduce the pain.

- Milky or snow; a gentle crystal that aids with meditation and promotes wisdom. This is a good meditation crystal which will help you to achieve a deep level of concentration and connection to your inner self. Like clear quartz it can be used as a general healing crystal but is gentler and slower to act.

Tiger's Eye

Another crystal that comes in a variety of colors, these beautiful and iridescent stones are flecked with luxuriant color. Tiger's eye has long been associated as a talisman stone, that protects and brings good luck. In general, the stone will bring feelings of self-worth and confidence. It both grounds and creates a sense of connection with the higher, spiritual world. Tiger's eye will, in general, bring good luck and is particularly associated with removing blockages in life.

- Blue; often a very dark bluish-green, this crystal brings enlightenment and confidence. This protective stone is used to find your true abilities and talents. In healing it is a good stone to help with cognitive disorders or for those who find it difficult to express themselves.

- Red; as with other red stones this crystal is linked with protection and also combat. This provides both self-knowledge and confidence; it's a stone that will help to banish fears or doubts and help the user to forge ahead in life. In healing it can be helped to overcome sexual difficulties and is also good for healing fatigue related illnesses.

Topaz

This popular gem is also an excellent crystal for use in healing. The delicate blue of topaz is linked to bright, clear skies and therefore to mental prowess and clarity of thought. It heals the spirit, creates openness to both others and to new concepts. It also promotes honesty, integrity and trust. Topaz can help to heal mental problems, anxiety and is a powerful stone for creating a deep link to the spiritual. Many healers choose this stone as their own, personal talisman to bring them strength and clarity in their work.

Turquoise

Like jade, this crystal has long been prized for its decorative and healing qualities. It is used to protect against negative influences from others and is also strongly associated with fresh, invigorating air. This makes it a useful stone in healing for dealing with breathing related disorders and lung problems. It can also have a deeply calming affect, making it useful for dealing with many issues including public speaking or to boost confidence in any venture. The clear, fresh nature of the gem sweeps away self-doubt and negative moods.

Conclusion

Thank you again for downloading this book!

I hope this book was able to help you understand the uses of crystals for healing.

The next step is to find the crystals that are right for you and use them to benefit your life and heal.

Finally, if you enjoyed this book, please take the time to share your thoughts and post a review on Amazon. It'd be greatly appreciated!

Thank you and good luck!

Preview of Chakras For Beginners

The ancient study of Chakras has made its way into the western world as of late. Frequently the first exposure can come through the study of yoga, meditation or hindu practices.

The body and every living being is filled with a universal energy that connects and surrounds us.This energy can has been described as being made up of 7 layers (Auras) and the 7 chakras (energy points or knots in the body)

This book is designed to offer a practical, usable introduction to the Chakras, how they can affect our health and well being and how to identify imbalances and address these.

The book is designed for those new to the concept but will also be useful for those with some experience of Chakra and energy healing. In the next chapter we take a more detailed look at what the Chakras are, and an overview of each one of the seven main Chakras. The remaining part of the book looks at each individual Chakra and how to examine the Chakra for imbalances. The final chapter provides a simple list-style section of tools that traditional (and modern) Chakra experts believe are useful in achieving balance within your Chakra energy system.

When our Chakras are in balance they allow energy to freely flow through our bodies and keep us revitalized, healthy and connected to the world around us. However, imbalances within the Chakra system can cause the energy to become blocked, leading to ill health both physical or emotional.

Here Is A Preview Of What You'll Learn...

- History Of Chakras
- What Chakras Are
- In-depth Description Of Each Chakra
- Causes Of Chakra Imbalances
- Chakra Test

- How To Balance Each Chakra

Get this book for a limited time offer of $2.99!

Check Out My Other Books

Below you'll find some of my other popular books that are popular on Amazon and Kindle as well.

Astrology: The Complete Guide To The Zodiac Signs

Numerology: The Ultimate Guide

Reiki: Reiki For Beginners

Spirit Guides: Spirit Guides For Beginners

About the Author

I want to thank you for giving me the opportunity to spend some time with you!
For the last 10 years of my life I have studied, practiced and shared my love of spirituality and internal development. I kept diaries for years documenting the incredible changes that graced my life. This passion for writing has blossomed into a new chapter in my life where publishing books has become a full time career.

I feel extremely blessed and fortunate to have the opportunity to share my message with you! Each of my books are written to inspire others to explore the many aspects of their internal world. My goal is to touch the lives of others in a positive way and hopefully be the catalyst of positive change in this world :)

I am forever grateful for your support and I know you will get immense value through my books. I am really looking forward to serve you and give you great insight into my passions!

Your Friend

Mia Rose

Printed in Great Britain
by Amazon

16892935R00020